Surviving Holidays, Birthdays, and Anniversaries: *a guide for grieving during special occasions*

A GRIEF STEPS GUIDE

www.griefsteps.com

adapted from I Wasn't Ready to Say Goodbye
by Brook Noel and Pamela D. Blair, Ph. D.

Also by Brook Noel & Pamela D. Blair, Ph.D.
I Wasn't Ready to Say Goodbye: surviving, coping and healing
    after the sudden death of a loved one
I Wasn't Ready to Say Goodbye Companion Workbook
Living with Grief: a guide for your first year of grieving

By Brook Noel
Back to Basics: 101 Ideas for Strengthening Our Children and
    Our Families
The Single Parent Resource
Surviving Holidays, Birthdays and Anniversaries: a guide for
    grieving during special occasions

Order online at www.championpress.com
or at www.griefsteps.com

CHAMPION PRESS, LTD.
FREDONIA, WISCONSIN
Copyright © 2003 Brook Noel

ISBN: 1891400037
Library of Congress Information Available Upon Request
Manufactured in the United States of America 10 9 8 7 6 5 4 3 2 1

This book is dedicated to my
"Champion Crew."
Wendy, Mike, Craig, Jim-2,
Mary Ann, Andy,
Samantha and Sara…
you make this all possible.
Thank you.

Table of Contents

Introduction: The Task of Mourning During Difficult Days........5

Chapter One: What to Expect During Difficult Days...........7

The Importance of Talking...8

Create A Space to Honor Your Feelings.........................10

Create A Group of Loved Ones......................................11

Choose Your Activities Wisely.......................................11

Help Others..12

Avoid Additional Stressors..12

Shop Online..13

Don't Try to Outspend Grief..13

Let Your Body Lead You..14

Don't Hide From Life..14

Beware of Self-Medicating..14

S.A.D..15

Chapter Two: The Ambush and Emotional Triggers............17

Understanding Emotional Triggers..................................21

Chapter Three: Strategies for Coping.............................24

Light a Candle...24

Write About It...24

Spread the Gifts..25

A Christmas Stocking..25

Honor the Holidays...25

Keep Your Faith..26

A Moment of Silence..26

Freewriting...27

Take a Time Out..27

Calming Exercise...28

Thank You Exercise...29

Memory Books...30

Chapter Four: Exploring Birthdays, Anniversaries & Weddings.34

Birthdays..34

Anniversaries..36

Weddings...39

Other Difficult Days...41

Chapter Five: Difficult Days: Holidays & Traditions.............42

Holiday Traditions...43

Where Does One Go During the Holidays............................46

Happy New Year...48

Next Year..50

Appendix A: A Guide for Those Helping Others with Grief......51

Grief Steps Support Site...55

Grief Steps Classes..56

Resources..59

Grief Guides...61

INTRODUCTION
The Task of Mourning During Difficult Days

"Grieving acknowledges and celebrates the union that you had with the person who died. It will help you reflect on his or her life and its impact on yours." *Carol Pack, Mayo Clinic Hospice Program*

Holidays, birthdays and other special days associated with the deceased present a special challenge. The loss becomes painfully evident and the feelings associated with the occasion become dulled and gray.

For most people, the holidays bring a time of joy and celebration. Family get-togethers, home-cooked dinners and family traditions surround us during these supposedly joyous times. Yet, for those who have experienced the loss of a loved one, the holidays are often robbed of their joy. Instead, these and other important days, carry loneliness and sadness. As we struggle with our sadness we are bombarded with happy family images through cards, television, store windows, movies, magazines and commercials. The contrasts between what we see and how we feel, only amplify our loneliness.

These days are especially difficult in the immediate years following our loss. Eventually, we will likely rediscover a new, although bittersweet joy, but at first this seems an incredibly hard task. In the beginning, our goal isn't to find happiness, but simply to survive and ease the loneliness we feel.

In this book we will explore what you can expect as you face these special days. When we are armed with knowledge, we can create a pathway for coping. The first two chapters offer an overview of the difficult days grievers face. In Chapters Three and Four we will explore some ideas and tactics you can use to ease the pain of these difficult times. And don't forget, there is always support a click away at www.griefsteps.com

CHAPTER ONE
What to Expect
During Difficult Days

As we first confront loss, almost every day is difficult. When we move from the initial stages of shock and mourning, the acute grief begins to lesson. We are not constantly locked in our grief, but we do find that it still surfaces—often around days filled with meaning.

This book is not intended to offer a pathway around the pain, but a pathway through the pain. Unfortunately, there isn't a magic route that allows us to sidestep the pain of grieving. Only by recognizing, confronting and facing our feelings can we get to the place where grief fades and we are left with cherished memories.

This book is intended to offer you strategies for coping. When we can anticipate the unexpected, we can prepare with ways to cope. After working with hundreds of people who have experienced loss in their lives, I have identified the most common setbacks and hurdles. Throughout this book we will explore these hurdles and strategies for leaping them. In later chapters we will explore the challenges brought on by specific holidays; but for now my goal is to arm you with an arsenal of techniques that can help you as you face your own difficult days.

Let's begin by exploring basic strategies that will help you throughout the grieving process.

The Importance of Talking

Perhaps the most important step toward healing is releasing our emotions and talking about our grief. With all the celebrations and happiness that surround us, we may feel awkward bringing up anything that isn't equally festive. But we must. We must release our feelings through talking to others. We must share what we have uncovered. If we don't, our feelings will lodge within us and create a dark sadness. The only way to get past our sadness is to move through it.

Make sure you have someone you can talk to about how you feel. If you do not have someone in your inner circle, consider a therapist, professional clergy person or joining a support group.

At first you will likely find yourself talking about the death over and over. As time passes, your conversation will focus more on the person you have lost until eventually you can begin to share the happy memories and times spent together.

Remember that our goal is not to erase the person we have lost, but to keep their memory alive in our everyday life. If we do not talk about our loved one, we cannot accomplish that goal.

It is also important to let those around us know that we want to talk about our loved one. In a world where few people know how to handle grief, many people think it painful to bring up the deceased's name. When you talk about your loved one, it serves as a signal to others that it is okay to share memories and thoughts.

In the Appendix, you will find a worksheet that can be photocopied and given to those who support you. The worksheet offers basic guidelines for helping someone who is grieving during the holidays.

Don't Let Anyone Tell You How to Grieve

Sometimes societal and religious beliefs impose rules such as time limits for grief, what we should wear, how we should behave, when and where we should talk about the death and to whom. It is important not to weight ourselves down with these societal expectations. We must find our own way to embrace life again. The acute grieving process often takes at least two years, while in other ways we never "get over" the loss completely. Our expression of grief is rooted in our need to make meaning or sense from what feels like meaningless tragedy, and no time limit can be set on that.

While friends may want you to "rejoin life," or "get past the loss," these are not judgments for friends to make. Only you can determine the time limits on your grief. Follow your heart and feelings when it comes to grieving—not the expectations of others.

Create A Space to Honor Your Feelings

Grief Sessions are set times when you honor your feelings. In our busy days we tend to immerse ourselves in activities (sometimes mindful, sometimes mindless) so we don't truly experience our grief. But we can't get through what we do not feel.

Some people find success in spending an hour taking a walk and getting in touch with their grief. Some people can sit outside with a journal and express their feelings. Just as our grief is unique, so will our Grief Sessions be equally unique. Write down some ideas for your own Grief Sessions—then schedule one on your calendar.

The goal of a Grief Session is simple. We set aside a fixed time where we are safe to experience our feelings. When we don't do this, we let our feelings build inside our hearts, only to cause further sadness and depression. We must expose our feelings and express them outwardly so that we may deal with them directly.

Consider setting up a quiet place in your home, perhaps with a candle and photograph of your loved one. At night, when the house is quiet, sit for a half hour in your special space and let your feelings rise to the surface. Many people report that journaling their feelings during these Grief Sessions can be extremely helpful.

Create A Group of Loved Ones

Chances are that other family members and friends who were close to the deceased will be having equal difficulty with these difficult days. Consider asking one or more people who are facing similar emotions, to gather for a support group. Perhaps you can meet for coffee once a week to discuss the challenges and emotions you are facing. You can also create a "phone support" system. Trade numbers so that in your times of pain you have someone you can reach out to. This works especially well if you are separated by many miles.

Choose Your Activities Wisely

During holidays and other busy seasons, not only do we have to face our grief, but we often have many other commitments and people that need our attention. There are presents to buy, parties to attend, preparations to make. As you look at the upcoming difficult days, take a personal "emotional inventory." Decide ahead of time how much you can handle. Then make sure you don't take on more than feels right for you.

Try not to feel guilty if you cannot do everything you once did during the holiday season. In time, you will get back "into the swing." This isn't the time to worry about keeping commitments—but a time to focus on keeping the commitment to your self to heal.

Help Others

Sometimes the easiest way to gain relief from grief is to help others who are in need. When we take our sadness and turn it into positive action, we can find meaning in our loss and the ability to focus on something other than our grief. Consider volunteering at a local charity. Let your loss inspire you to help others.

Avoid Additional Stressors

Even when not facing grief, the holidays bring added stress for many. Between all the tasks to be done and the variety of expectations, our bodies, hearts, and minds are often taxed to their limit. As you access the upcoming days, think of things you can do now to avoid later stress. Can you pay your bills a month early making them one less thing to worry about? If you will need a babysitter, can you arrange for that now? If you have travel plans, can you book your hotel and tickets prior to the start of the holiday season? Any steps we can take to reduce additional stressors are steps in the right direction.

Shop Online

The thought of navigating crowds to purchase gifts intimidates many grievers. If you aren't ready to face the camaraderie of the holidays, do your shopping online or from catalogs. Another option is to place cash in gift cards or use gift certificates.

Don't Try to Outspend Grief

As you face your holiday shopping, beware of the common pitfall of trying to "outspend" your grief. When we are feeling a hole or ache inside, human nature often leads us to purchase items to fill that void. This urge is like a drug, offering temporary relief that will quickly fade and leave a bigger hole in its wake. It's great to purchase a special 'treat" for yourself over the holidays, just don't get carried away with shopping as a way to lesson grief's grip.

Let Your Body Lead You

Grief affects each one of us differently. Some of us may become very active and busy, while others may become lethargic or practically comatose. Let your body lead you. If you feel tired—sleep. If you feel like crying—cry. If you are hungry—eat. Don't feel you need to act one way or another. There are no "shoulds" right now, simply follow the lead of your body.

Don't Hide From Life

It can be tempting to isolate ourselves from others when we are filled with sadness. We may feel like it takes too much energy to engage with others or that people just "won't understand how we feel." Regardless of the effort it takes, it is very important to spend time with other people. Talking and sharing (even when not grief-related) are necessary steps in helping to rejoin with society and to adjust to our loss. Isolating one's self from others will only cause deeper sadness.

Beware of Self-Medicating

Some grievers use, or increase their use, of alcohol or antidepressants. Abusing food is another common 'attempt to escape' since most holiday festivities bring loads of rich foods. When we do this, we distance ourselves from what we need to feel to heal, and we distance ourselves from our family members and support systems as well. Our grief simply goes underground and waits to be expressed. We may mistakenly believe that "If I drink (drug or eat) to get over it, then the grief will be gone when I'm sober." Nothing could be further from the truth. The sadness awaits us, often stronger and deeper than before we attempted self-medication.

SAD

In addition to the already complicated task of mourning, there is another complexity to the holiday season. Many people suffer from depression in the winter months. This depression is called Seasonal Affective Disorder (SAD). Research has shown that decreased sunlight can cause depression in some people. Currently, about 11 million people suffer from this form of depression and women are four times more likely to suffer than men.

If prior to your loss, you experienced a sense of "holiday blues" you may have been suffering from SAD. Consider a professional diagnosis and treatment to help rid this unnecessary pain and complication.

Many people also report a post-holiday blues. Along with the stress that the holidays bring while we are grieving, they also bring mandatory contact with many people. When the holiday season passes and January comes, many people again feel increased sadness or depression. This may be another indication of SAD or a post-seasonal depression. If this describes you, make sure to schedule an appointment with your doctor. Medical technology has advanced significantly and there are many options for treatment that carry few side effects.

CHAPTER TWO
The Ambush
and Emotional Triggers

In today's world we have grown accustomed to scheduling so much of life. Most of us own at least one organizer or appointment book. Yet grief is one emotion that will never fit in an appointment-square. You may find there are times when you are in the midst of a normal, pleasant activity and suddenly a wash of grief comes over you. Know that this is common and that grief can surface at any time, without notice. I experienced this grief, which I call the "ambush" while watching television...

"I remember watching a television comedy with my husband. I had been laughing throughout the show and it had been a while since I had shed tears over my brother's death. Then there was an ad to solicit funds for needy children—the theme song was *Amazing Grace.*

The day before we cremated Caleb, we had held a small viewing for his closest friends and family. We had given the pastor no instruction and the pastor sang that song.

I had been driven to tears then, and I was driven to tears again as I watched the ad on television. A year and a half later, I was walking on Bourbon Street in New Orleans when again I heard a street performer singing *Amazing Grace*. I had tears in my eyes then as well."

My friend Pam had a similar experience...

"George was a Beatles fan. Many months after he died, while in a fast food restaurant and mid-bite of my hamburger, the piped-in music started with John Lennon's *Imagine* and a nail went into my heart."

There is so little of life we control. Grief's timing is among the uncontrollable. Expect experiences, similar to these, frequently over the first three to six months (the frequency is often based on how close you were to the deceased). Over the course of a year, they will lessen, but they may still happen from time to time.

Many grievers are surprised by the "ambush." I want to take a moment to explain what an ambush is and how it surfaces during our grieving.

Ambushes are particularly evident around special occasions such as birthdays, anniversaries, and holidays, or any time you are expected to participate in a celebration of some kind. They can also surface without any noticeable or predictable cause as we move through our days.

An ambush brings deep pain and sadness, as if the death had just occurred, Just when you think you're coping fine, along comes the dreaded ambush! Up from "no where" the rage resurfaces, the disbelief, the flashback, the horror, the insane feeling, the heightened awareness. These situations often occur just when you tell yourself, and your friends, "I'm finally beginning to feel better."

Odds are you have already experienced an ambush. Perhaps a song you heard on the radio triggered a flood of memories. You may know exactly what kind of place or event triggers you (i.e. a particular store in the mall, the sound of children playing, the smell of pizza, a certain sporting event...) and you can choose to avoid those situations. However, sometimes the unavoidable occurs—the tears begin to flow and the outrage returns. My co-author of *I Wasn't Ready to Say Goodbye,* Pamela D. Blair, had this type of experience.

"I remember going to the supermarket and seeing my loved one's favorite Campbells™ soup on the shelf. I dissolved into tears and the mascara ran in streams onto to my white blouse. You might try wearing sunglasses in public. I did and it helped disguise the red, puffy eyes and the raccoon look. I also carried tissues and told strangers that I was dealing with a lousy allergy attack. And sometimes I told the truth."

If practical, when you experience an ambush, stop what you are doing and honor your emotions. Have the feeling, weep the tears, beat the pillows, phone someone (or everyone) in your support group. Allow the pain to wash through you and deliberately allow it to have its full force.

A word of caution—if the "ambush" occurs while you are driving a car or other vehicle, pull over where it is safe. Driving with tears in your eyes and rage in your heart can be hazardous.

As you face your grief, it is almost impossible to avoid the occasional ambush. Know that these "emotional floods" are normal. Understanding your unique "emotional triggers" can help you anticipate an ambush. It is also helpful to decide in advance on a strategy for coping. Many of the exercises in Chapter Three will be useful.

Understanding Emotional Triggers

Like most feelings, ambushes have a cause. By paying attention and doing a little "ground work" we can learn to identify these personal emotional triggers that create such complicated emotions within us.

It is not only important to identify the emotions we are feeling, but to understand how these emotions affect us. It can be helpful to keep a journal documenting your "emotional triggers." Use your journal as a sort of "field study" to document how the formula you'll learn below affects your thoughts, feelings, moods and actions.

Cognitive experts have determined that what we think about creates our feelings, our feelings create our moods, and our moods fuel our actions. In its most basic sense the equation looks like this:

Thoughts = feelings,
which = moods, which = actions
therefore   *Thoughts = Actions*

When we work this equation in reverse, we can see where our actions stem from. First, take an action and ask yourself what type of mood you were in when you did the action. Then ask yourself what feelings led to that mood. Lastly, ask yourself what thoughts you were thinking. Each of these steps can be documented in your journal.

Let's look at an example. One holiday season I found myself continually over-eating. I had never been one to eat past the point of fullness and suddenly I became an insatiable hole that no amount of food could fill. So the action I would be working with is "perpetual overeating throughout the holidays." Then I needed to ask myself what mood I was in. I can remember feeling depressed. Then I needed to ask myself what feelings led to that mood. I remember feeling very lonely. Lastly, I examined my thoughts. I remember thinking about how much I missed my brother, and others who I have loved and lost over the years.

By re-reading the above exercise, I can find several places where I have an opportunity to change what was happening. (1) I could prevent the loneliness by talking about my losses with others. (2) I could have spent less time in isolation and more time with people who are important to me. (3) When I felt lonely, I could have reached out to a support person. Any of these three steps would have likely changed the eventual outcome of perpetual overeating resulting in a more healthy form of grieving.

This process may be tenuous at first, but the more often it is done, the easier it becomes. This is an excellent way to get in touch with our thoughts and feelings, to see how they affect our lives. You may even choose to explore this formula with the happy moments in your life. When you can identify the correlation between your thoughts, feelings, moods and actions you can repeat the patterns that give you pleasure and decrease the patterns that bring you pain.

Once you have done this exercise for awhile, you will be able to recognize these emotional triggers. When you recognize a thought process, you will know the mood and action that is likely to follow. Knowing this gives you the opportunity to change your thoughts and thus change your eventual action. This process is where the cliché, "Change your mind, change your life," stems from.

CHAPTER THREE
Strategies for Coping

Beyond the ambushes and understanding our emotional triggers, there are many ways to cope with the sadness brought on by holiday grief. In this chapter we will explore ways to cope and move toward healing. Not every exercise and suggestion will work for you, but some of them will. Be open to trying each exercise once to see how it can benefit you. Then make a list, in your journal, of those choices that are most beneficial for you. Use those to help you cope as you face your difficult days.

Light a Candle
Select a beautifully scented candle. Throughout your difficult days, light the candle as a reminder of your bond with the person you have lost. Let the light of the candle offer you comfort. You may want to spend a certain amount of time near the candle recalling pleasant memories or writing in your journal.

Write About It
Shakespeare said, "Give sorrow words..." and for thousands of years words have offered solace to those who are grieving. Consider writing a story about

your loss or a story about your loved one. Try writing a poem or a song. Don't worry about form or grammar—just let the words flow. You'll find additional writing exercises under "freewriting" in this chapter. You may also want to explore the online course I offer on my web site Grief Steps, titled *Writing through Grief.* This six-week, online, interactive course is a great way to begin the writing process.

Spread the Gifts

Use the money that you would have spent on gifts for your loved one to make a special donation to charity in his or her honor.

A Christmas Stocking

Consider hanging a stocking for your loved one. Ask family members to write about a favorite moment or special memory and place it in the stocking. Spend an evening sharing these "stocking memories."

Honor the Holidays

If you have access to the cemetery or burial site of your loved one, consider placing a holiday wreath or sprig of holly at the site. Spend some time at the gravesite 'talking' to your loved one.

Keep Your Faith

If you have attended religious services in the past, try to continue to do so. Many grievers report finding solace or feeling the presence of the one they have lost inside the serenity of these services.

A Moment of Silence

When the actual difficult day arrives, you may find the celebration awkward. It may feel as though people are not sure how to act around you. Should they try to spread their holiday cheer or should they try to comfort you? Many people don't do either as we live in a society where people often don't know how to help those who are hurting—they want to make all the pain go away—and that is impossible.

If you find this to be the case at your celebration, consider asking for a moment of silence before the meal. Express your thanks for being with everyone, and ask for a moment to remember the one you have lost. This helps to bring the topic of loss 'to the table" and will let people know that you are okay with talking about your loss; in fact for many grievers, it is helpful. You could also ask people to share a favorite story after dinner. Let your feelings guide you toward what will be most comforting.

Freewriting: Freewriting is the process of recording thoughts and feelings on the fly. Instead of analyzing what you are writing or worrying about form and structure, you just write continually. There are only two rules for freewriting—you can't stop moving your pen or pencil—and you can't erase anything you have written. The point is to dig past the surface and into your soul—and then to give your soul a space to express itself. Freewriting works especially well for those who are intimidated by the thought of journaling. It can also be used in conjunction with journaling. I recommend a five minute freewrite first thing in the morning. When we first wake, we can access our innermost thoughts more readily. If you are leery about trying a freewrite, that is all the more reason to push yourself to do so. You might find that this can help you uncover much of your inner life. Try to make a commitment to write at least four mornings each week for five minutes. Set a timer for yourself. When the timer dings, stop writing.

Take a Time Out
Make sure to leave some "emotional space" in your schedule for a 'time out.' Special days are naturally taxing and stressful and are compounded by grief. Allow yourself some time to decompress.

Calming Exercise

Stress, anxiety, sadness, depression—these emotions can leave us knotted inside. Practicing deep breathing exercises can help us to relax and unwind our wound-up-emotions. The following exercises will help calm you during trying times.

Place one hand on your abdomen. As you inhale, you want to feel the movement in your abdomen, not in your chest. Inhale for the count of ten, then exhale for the count of ten. Repeat this ten to fifteen times for deeper relaxation.

To relax your whole body, lay down in a quiet place. Breathe deeply, slowly inhaling and exhaling. Beginning with your left leg, clench your muscles as tightly as you can for the count of three. Then relax them. Do the same with the right leg, left arm and right arm. Then move up your body tightening your pelvis, then stomach, then chest, then shoulders, then neck and lastly facial muscles. When you have completed this exercise you should feel extremely calm and peaceful. Visualize an ocean beach or other calming scene to deepen the relaxing experience.

Thank You Exercise

As you continue to grow and heal you will eventually discover at least something (no matter how seemingly insignificant) for which you can express gratitude. If the expression is not available to you now, realize that it is a temporary condition.

After you have honored your anger, and when you are ready, you might want to try this Thank You Exercise. Compared to all other acts, personal and spiritual growth is greatest through the expression of gratitude. No matter how difficult at first, expressing appreciation for your loss can help make some meaning in the face of tragedy. Acknowledging, in writing, what was empowering and uplifting, will help you retain what was valuable and will help you to let go of the false belief that you cannot grow or learn after your loss.

Why pick up a pen and write a note? Why not? Just think about it. The act of writing, choosing the type of pen and paper, the color of the ink, moving the pen across the paper, seeing the words—all make what you are saying more real—more concrete. You will notice your energy shift—from confusion about what to write; anger at having to sort through your life for the first time (or the thousandth time); your tears as you recognize what you have lost; and ultimately, a sense of relief at having given yourself the chance to express the unsaid.

Date and save your notes in a special place or put them in your journal. You may want to destroy a note, but remember, this is about expressing feelings that need to be expressed. Rereading them again, after several months or years can be useful, so you may want to save them for future reference. It is also useful to write another note after some time has passed. Each time you write, you will gain new insights. If you have young children you may even want to read your journal to them when they are older.

Memory Books

Creating a memory book is a wonderful keepsake about our loved one. When Brook's brother died, she collected articles, photos and other memorabilia to put in a keepsake album. Using different papers, stencils, markers and stickers she created special pages to "frame" her memories.

Album making has become popular in recent years. Many scrapbooking stores now exist that offer classes on how to archive our memories creatively. Through collage, rubber stamping, paper decorations and other means, we can make a beautiful book to serve as a remembrance.

In addition to stores that can serve as creative outlets, many magazines and books offer guidance. Even if you don't consider yourself creative, there are tools to help you get started. Check the craft section of your local bookstore for books on scrapbooking. A large newsstand or craft store may carry magazines such as *Memory Makers* and *Somerset Studio*, which offer ideas.

There are also consultants for companies like D.O.T.S. and Creative Memories that sell supplies and can help you choose your materials, while offering creative guidance. Check your yellow pages for these companies. Current is another great source for materials. They can be accessed on the Internet at http://www.current.com

Here are a few basic tips for building your memory book.

1. Choose a quality album to hold your memories. Creative Memories and D.O.T.S. both offer wonderful albums. Also make sure to use acid-free papers and supplies whenever possible. When papers are acid-free, they will not damage your photographs or yellow over time.

2. Collect all the materials that you think you would like to include. The possibilities are endless—postcards, words clipped from

magazines, photos, special poems—anything that you like can be included.

3. Sort the items you have gathered until you see a natural progression taking form. You may want to move through the book chronologically, or another theme may occur to you.

4. Gather stencils, stickers, stamps and papers to use as decorations. Craft and scrapbooking stores are obvious suppliers. Additionally, office-supply stores and stores like K-Mart, Wal-Mart and Target often have good selections at reasonable prices.

5. Choose the materials you would like to use for a given page. Lay them out and move them around until you are comfortable with the design. If you have problems coming up with ideas for layout, consult one of the aforementioned magazines.

6. Take your time. There is no need to try and rush through the process of creating a memory book. Many people find joy in the "putzing" and creating. It may be a book that

you will continually add to throughout your
lifetime.

Chapter Four
Exploring Birthdays,
Anniversaries & Weddings

Birthdays

The deceased person's birthday is a time for remembering. You may feel your loss anew each time their birthday comes for many years. There is a strange feeling that arises as we age--while our loved one seems "frozen in time" at whatever age they were when they died. I remember how odd it felt to turn 28. My older brother had died at age 27. It felt very uncomfortable to be "older" than my "older brother." These dynamics make the grieving of birthdays especially difficult.

Chapter Three contains many ideas that can be used to honor your loved one during their birthday. Here are a few others that may add meaning to this special day...

1. Enjoy a birthday dinner with a friend at one of your loved one's favorite places. Choose a friend with whom you can share memories and stories.

2. Give a special gift to a charity or someone in need, in honor of your loved one's birthday.

3. Make a wonderful birthday cake and enjoy a slice while "talking" to your loved one. Remember, it is perfectly okay and healthy to have a relationship with your loved one after death. Death signifies the end of their time in human form on earth, but it need not signify the end of your connection.

4. Look through albums of past birthdays and recollect fond memories.

5. Write a birthday note to your loved one in your journal. On a quiet and calm night, take it outside and read it aloud. Look up at the stars. Find comfort in the vastness of the universe and its mysteries.

Not only will your loved one's birthday feel different, but your own birthday may seem different. You may wonder why you are still alive and they are not, and it will be difficult to celebrate your own life for a while.

Many people find sanctuary by creating a ritual with which to celebrate the deceased's birthday. Perhaps you can surround yourself with other people who were close to the loved one. Or perhaps you'll choose to take a walk in nature and just think and cry and rant and talk. Look through the ideas for coping in Chapter Three for additional ways to honor this special day.

Anniversaries

Some people find that they may do well for an entire year, only to find themselves virtually incapacitated by grief during the days surrounding the anniversary of the death. You wake up one morning with a heavy feeling, not realizing exactly why you feel so burdened. Then it hits you—the anniversary of a special date you shared with the deceased in the past or the anniversary of the death itself.

On the anniversary of the day of death, many grievers report a short-term depression. It is not uncommon to annually experience discomfort, sadness and depression for a couple weeks before and after the date of death. For my family, when the leaves begin to change color, a short-term depression starts almost immediately. It was October 4th when my brother died and in Wisconsin the leaves begin to turn near the end of September.

The strength of a support network can be beneficial during this time. Many people do "fine" throughout the year, only to be knocked off their feet as these significant dates occur.

Some religious traditions have a requirement around the one year anniversary of the death. In Judaism for instance, Judaic law has a prescribed ritual for "death days"—the anniversary of the death. You are expected to need to discharge extra emotions during these days. The headstone is unveiled at this time. Even if your religious tradition does not dictate it, you will feel some deep or extreme emotion on the anniversary of the death. Try to look at the anniversary of the death as another opportunity to grieve—to feel some of what has been unexpressed up until now.

It is also helpful to decide in advance how you want to spend the anniversary of the death. For the first two years after my brother's death, I felt the need to go somewhere in nature and spend the day and night alone. Today, as I am writing this, it Is October 4, 2003, 6 years after my brother's death. I am with my family in a hotel in the Wisconsin Dells. My brother was a very talented water-skier and was honored with a special plaque which we have yet to see. Later today, my mother and I are going to go see it. I noticed that even though we still miss him incredibly, we are definitely able to laugh more now. The pain is still there, but it is a bittersweet pain, instead of just a bitterness.

As the years pass, our needs will change. This year you may need to spend the day alone while next year you may find comfort in a group or with family. Be open to your evolving needs.

Other anniversaries where you can expect to feel "extra emotions" include:
the last day you saw your loved one alive
the day you first met
the day you were married or engaged
the day the "plug" was pulled
the day you found out they were dead
the anniversary of a trip you took together

Of course there will be others depending on your relationship to the deceased. If you expect these anniversaries to be challenging emotional times you will be less surprised. If you know they are coming, and when, you will be better able to cope. If you can, make special arrangements for yourself (i.e. take the day off from work, get a baby-sitter for the kids, find time and space to be alone, visit the grave, etc.). You may want to consider a ritual for the day of death. Use the ideas and exercises throughout this book as a springboard for rituals.

Weddings

If you are mourning the loss of a spouse, weddings can be especially difficult to attend. The bride and groom look so happy, "don't they know it can be all over in a matter of seconds!" The vows are said and you hear "until death do us part," and then the tears well up. If you have lost a young daughter or son, expect to feel anger and sadness that you will never see them marry, and that you will not have grandchildren, etc. If you are in the early stages of mourning, it may be better for you to stay away from wedding ceremonies altogether and attend receptions instead. Or send a gift and stay home. This is a day of celebration for the bride and groom and their families. They may avoid you in an effort to maintain their joy and experience of the celebration. Try not to take their actions personally.

If you are the one getting married, expect your wedding day to be filled with a flood of emotions. Anger might be one of them—"Mom was supposed to be here, sitting in the front row. Now I have to look at an empty chair. It's not fair!"—"My sister was to be maid of honor." "My best friend was looking forward to being my best man!" Your anger and sadness may seem unbearable. Make sure this is the right time for your wedding and you wouldn't be better served by pushing it back a bit. Everyone will understand with the grief you are facing.

You can also be creative in your wedding if it will help to honor your loved one and bring you peace. My brother's best friend, Rob, was scheduled to get married shortly after my brother's death. He would have chosen Caleb as his best man. With Caleb unable to be there, he asked me to be his best man. Although I looked a bit funny in a tux, it was a great memory as I became his "Best Man-ly Woman."

Expect to have some tears—for joy and for sadness. Make sure you tuck a tissue in your bouquet or your jacket pocket. Let the officiant know what you are going through ahead of time. It would also be appropriate to ask the officiant to honor your lost loved one by requesting a moment of silence during the ceremony, as you light a candle for you missing loved one.

Pam, in her role as Interfaith Minister, does many wedding ceremonies. The following is an excerpt from one wedding where the bride had experienced a recent loss. You may wish to incorporate these words or something similar into your own ceremony:

> *As we light these candles, we sense the love and the presence of all those who have gone before us—especially Denise's mother, Ruth. We feel her with us today, adding her special blessing to this sacred ceremony. It is my hope and my prayer that the families*

of Denise and Michael, both seen and
unseen, will do all they can to help sustain
and nurture the bond of these two as they
seek to create their own family.

Other Difficult Days

While anniversaries, weddings, birthdays and holidays are easily identifiable days, there are other days that often cause our grief to rise to the surface. For many, time as we once knew it ceases to exist. Instead of four seasons and twelve months, grievers often tell time in relationship to their loss. We are acutely aware of the day our loved one died. We count the year from this date...*two months have passed since he died....this is the first start of football season since he died...the first school concert since we lost our loved one.* Each day can take on significant meaning as it becomes the first time we confront a situation without our loved one.

Understand that it is natural to look at the world differently now. You are seeing the world with new eyes and through a new experience. In time you will not hold a magnifying glass to the calendar. For now, remember you are a new person, taking tentative steps in a new world. There will be many falls—but you will learn to walk again—and eventually enjoy the walk.

CHAPTER FIVE
Difficult Days: Holidays & Traditions

With the loss of a member of your immediate family, holidays and special occasions will be difficult. Holidays are often filled with traditions and memories of closeness. As we face these days without our loved one, the empty space looms large in our hearts. By creating new traditions and by understanding the common difficulties faced during the holidays, these difficult days can be easier to cope with.

The American Association of Retired Persons offers these tips in their article, "Frequently Asked Questions by the Widowed."

☐ **Plan ahead.** It helps to ease the strain.

☐ **Set priorities.** This can make it easier to phase out elements less pleasing to you.

☐ **Make new traditions.** This new phase in your life deserves some new traditions.

☐ **Include [the deceased's] name in conversation.** It helps others talk about him/her.

- ☐ **Express your feelings.** Most people understand and accept your need to cry.

- ☐ **Find someone you can help.** Giving assistance to others is very satisfying.

- ☐ **Buy yourself something special.** You've suffered a great loss. Be good to yourself.

- ☐ **Cherish your memories.** These are yours to keep; they grow more precious over time.

- ☐ **Be patient with yourself.** Allow yourself extra time to accomplish tasks.

- ☐ **Take time out for rest and relaxation.** This will ease the stress of grief."

Most importantly, take your time and be gentle with yourself as you move through the holidays.

Holiday Traditions

Don't try to hold on to the way things were done in the past with your previous traditions. Your family has changed. It's okay to change the way you celebrate the holidays as well.

Many grievers report that they find solace in some of their traditions, while others feel awkward or cause sadness. Hold onto the traditions that comfort you, but set the others aside. Think of a new tradition. If you always celebrated Christmas at home, consider renting a cabin for a couple of days. If you always put your tree up early in the season, consider putting it up later. If a large dinner was always cooked, go out for dinner instead. Do things differently. The memories will be strong when the holidays come; altering a routine is the best way to still find some joy. My family changed our routine after the unexpected death of my brother...

"Caleb died two months prior to Christmas. Both my mother and I had done most of our shopping. As Christmas neared and we were still heavily immersed in sadness, we wondered what to do with all the gifts. We decided to give them to Caleb's friends. To change our routine, instead of celebrating Christmas day at my mothers', she came down to my house in southern Wisconsin. Now, she comes out to my Portland home each year. While we always have Caleb in our minds and hearts, we have learned the need to let go of some of the pain and engage in activities and new traditions that can help us move forward with our lives."

When you do as I did, you are honoring your lost loved one. It may seem as though we are disrespecting our loved ones or moving away from our memories—but in fact, we are paying tribute by moving on with our lives. Elizabeth was a newly widowed mother when the holidays came. She shares her story...

"The holidays, oh please save me from the holidays...make them go away! I remember my thoughts as a newly widowed mother of two young children sixteen years ago, as I raced around trying to put some kind of Thanksgiving and Christmas together. *Can't we just forget about it this year? Doesn't the rest of the world know how much pain I'm in?* I got together with another sad and lonely woman from my support group. I invited her and her kids to my house to have a turkey dinner for Thanksgiving. It helped to not face the carving of the turkey (which he did, rather poorly each year) alone. Somehow I did it, whatever "it" was, all the while listening to the happy Christmas carolers, fa la la la, la, la, la la.

Christmas day that first year was really strange. I opened the presents with my two children and then sat staring at the tree, imagining how it would feel to hurl the decorations off the deck and set the living room on fire. I must have sat in the green living room chair for two hours after that, not moving."

Where Does One Go During the Holidays?

Does one have to go anywhere? Do you have to pretend to be happy and joyous for the sake of others? Is it okay to celebrate or not to celebrate this year if you want to? Like so much of the grief process, we need to listen to our inner guidance in these matters. If you need to be alone, that's okay. You can choose that. You may have to put something together for your kids and that's fine. You may even find them a great joy, an inspiration and a reason to get out of bed. Other than the practical needs of those who are dependent upon you, you don't need to take care of others by pretending "everything is all right."

If you do visit family and friends during the holidays, feel free to let them know the following ahead of time:

- I may need to leave your home earlier than you expect me to. (I get tired easily these days because I'm under a lot of stress.)

- I may need to take a walk by myself after dinner. (It's hard to be around happy families for too long a time.)
- I may cry unexpectedly when I hear certain music. (I have memories of good times and it's hard to hold back the tears.)
- I may not eat all the food and goodies you offer me. (My appetite hasn't been what it used to be—maybe I'm finding all this "hard to swallow.")

Even without a sudden death in your family or close circle of friends, the holidays can bring on many difficult feelings. Depression is the most difficult feeling of all. You will need to face the fact that it's going to be nearly impossible to stave off this seasonal depression. Everyone "seems" to be so happy; families are gathering together while there is a void in your life. Walking through the mall you may see the perfect gift for your deceased loved one and dissolve into a flood of tears. You may have already bought the deceased gifts and there they sit, wrapped, under the tree, unopened. It would be extremely arrogant of us to suggest there is an easy fix for the kind of depression that surfaces around the holidays. Both authors still suffer from periodic holiday blues. It may provide some relief to volunteer your time to help the needy and hungry. Giving of yourself to another, less fortunate person or to someone who has experienced a similar loss can take your mind off your own sadness—for a time.

This year, be one of the first people you think about during the holiday season. A support group will be especially useful during this trying time of year. Peers can offer rituals and ideas that they use to make the holidays easier, or they can offer a shoulder to lean on in your time of need.

Happy New Year?

You may be at a different place right now and your optimism about the future may have started to return. Celebrate! You are moving along in your recovery. For others, especially those in the early stages of recovery (first, second and third year), optimism about anything is a struggle. The first full year without your loved one can be especially difficult. Your well-meaning friends and relatives may have a different opinion. You may hear phrases like, "It's the New Year—time for you to start fresh, get a new lease on life, stop crying and feeling sorry for yourself." It is important to remember when confronted with their judgments or concerns that *your* recovery is *your* recovery. *Your* time frame for healing is *your* time frame, not theirs.

You may simply need to acknowledge that it is a new year and leave it at that. If the death occurred two years ago, you may mistakenly believe that since you are now two years into recovery you *should* be feeling better by now. Don't be fooled by dates.

It's possible the thought of a New Year's Eve celebration (or any celebration for that matter) will bring up deep sadness surrounding the loss of good times with the deceased or perhaps memories that are less than pleasant (i.e. drunkenness and unsafe driving). In either case, it is important to honor yourself wherever you are. You might make up your own New Year ritual—light some candles (one for each month/year you have made it on your own), burn some incense (to symbolize the burning away of the old way of being and the sweet smell of a new way), pour yourself a glass of wine or soda and drink a toast to yourself. You may have begun to live! It might be a good time to compare where you are emotionally with where you were last year at this time. Last year you may have wanted to stay in bed with the covers over your head every day of the week, and maybe now you only think about staying in bed three days a week—without the covers pulled up! These are not small steps. They are large strides on the path of grief recovery and they deserve your praise and recognition.

Next Year

Next year it will hurt a little less—next year there will be a little more joy in your life. Next year you may be able to hear the music. Next year you may have more to give. Next year you may even be more ready to help someone else. Wherever you are in the grief process, there is the possibility of new life. We know it's hard—and we also know it gets less hard. The next time a special occasion, anniversary or holiday comes around you will feel a little more in control, a little less pained, the situation will be a little less difficult and you will begin to celebrate life again—one day at a time, one year at a time.

APPENDIX A

HOW TO HELP SOMEONE WHO IS GRIEVING DURING THE HOLIDAYS

A Guide for Those Helping Others with Grief
(photocopy and give to close
friends and loved ones)

Don't try to find the magic words or formula to eliminate the pain. Nothing can erase or minimize the painful tragedy your friend or loved one is facing. Your primary role at this time is simply to "be there." Don't worry about what to say or do, just be a presence that the person can lean on when needed. Even though the holidays are meant to be a happy time, respect that the holidays will be difficult for the person who is grieving. Don't try to overly spread the holiday spirit—instead, respect the emotions and feelings that are conveyed to you.

Don't try to minimize or make the person feel better. When we care about someone, we hate to see them in pain. Often we'll say things like, "I know how you feel," or "perhaps, it was for the best," in order to minimize their hurt. While this can work in some instances, it never works with grief.

Help with responsibilities. Even though a life has stopped, our lives do not. One of the best ways to help is to run errands, prepare food, take care of the kids, do laundry and help with the simplest of maintenance. The holidays always carry extra responsibilities. See if you can help with shopping, Christmas cards or any other holiday needs.

Don't expect the person to reach out to you. Many people say, "call me if there is anything I can do." At this stage, the person who is grieving will be overwhelmed at the simple thought of picking up a phone. If you are close to this person, simply stop over and begin to help. People need your help but may be too depleted to ask. There are many friends that will be with you during the good times—but few that are there in life's darkest hour, when friendship and sensitivity are most needed.

Talk through decisions. While working through the grief process many bereaved people report difficulty with decision making. Be a sounding board for your friend or loved one and help them think through their decisions.

Don't be afraid to say the name of the deceased.
Those who have lost someone usually speak of them often, and believe it or not, need to hear the deceased's name and stories. In fact, it is estimated that 98% of grievers welcome talking about the loved one.

Remember that time does not heal all wounds.
Your friend or loved one will change because of what has happened. Everyone grieves differently. Some will be "fine" and then experience their true grief a year later, others grieve immediately. There are no timetables, no rules—be patient.

Remind the bereaved to take care of themselves.
Eating, resting and self-care are all difficult tasks when besieged by the taxing emotions of grief. You can help by keeping the house stocked with healthy foods that are already prepared (or easy-to-prepare). Help with the laundry. Take over some errands so the bereaved can rest. However, do not push the bereaved to do things they may not be ready for. Many grievers say, "I wish they would just follow my lead." While it may be upsetting to see the bereaved withdrawing from people and activities—it is normal. They will rejoin as they are ready.

Avoid judging. Don't tell the person how to react or handle their emotions or situation. Simply let him/her know that you support their decisions and will help in any way possible.

Share a Meal. Invite the bereaved over regularly to share a meal or take a meal to their home since meal times can be especially lonely. Consider inviting the bereaved out on important dates like the one-month anniversary of the death, the deceased's birthday, or other occasions meaningful to the griever.

Make a list of everything that needs to be done with the bereaved. This could include everything from bill paying to plant watering. Prioritize these by importance. Help the bereaved complete as many tasks as possible. If there are many responsibilities, find one or more additional friends to support you.

Make a personal commitment to help the one grieving get through this. After a death, many friendships change or disintegrate. People don't know how to relate to the one who is grieving, or they get tired of being around someone who is sad. Vow to see your friend or loved one through this, to be their anchor in their darkest hour.

Excerpted from "I Wasn't Ready to Say Good-bye: a guide for surviving, coping and healing with the sudden death of a loved one by Brook Noel and Pamela D. Blair, Ph.D. ISBN 1-891400-27-4, Champion Press, Ltd.

a caring community for those living with loss

Grief Steps.Com Offering 24/7 Support

Grief Steps is a program created by best-selling author Brook Noel, to reach out and provide support to the many people experiencing loss in their lives. Noel created www.griefsteps.com to offer 24/7, free internet support to anyone needing assistance during loss.

Joining is Free and Simple

Simply log onto www.griefsteps.com You will find support chats, support e-mail groups, a reading room, a free newsletter and other support services. Membership is free and the support is there for you—as little or as much as you need.

Take a step toward healing with interactive, online courses led by best-selling author Brook Noel

How do the classes work?

Its easy to get started with a GriefSteps class. Simply enroll in the course of your choice at www.griefsteps.com We offer a wide variety of classes ranging in price from $19 to $129.

What do I get with my class?

1. Once you enroll, you'll receive a welcome packet that will contain directions for the course.

2. Each class has "assignments" that you can turn in for comments from Brook Noel.

3. Each class also has a message board where you can post questions and talk to other students.

4. Each class includes a designated weekly, one-hour "chat" time. You can log on to the private chat to talk about your experiences and assignments. These chats are moderated by Brook Noel.

*Participation in chats, message boards and assignments is optional.

Healing Exercises – Part One

In this interactive, online course, you'll complete 10 different exercises that help you move forward through grief and resolve open issues. These exercises can be completed again and again after the class to further your healing. Brook Noel will comment on work you choose to turn in and encourage you in your journey.

Class length – 6 weeks   Cost $49

Now What? Living After Loss

This class offers a solid foundation for anyone wondering how to go on after loss. You'll learn what to expect physically and emotionally and how to take your first steps toward healing.

Class length – 3 weeks   Cost $19

Rituals to Honor Your Loved One

Rituals are a wonderful way to keep the memory of your loved one with you. This class will introduce you to different types of rituals and guide you in creating one of your own.

Class length – 4 weeks   Cost $29

When Will the Pain End?
Working through Unresolved Grief

Throughout this 10 week course, you'll learn about the different stages of grief and how to recognize which of your life losses have not been grieved completely. You'll learn exercises and tactics to heal and work through unresolved grief issues, which are the most common causes of sadness and depression. This is the perfect class for anyone who is having difficulty moving forward after a life loss.

Class length – 10 weeks   Cost $99

The Healing Journey: Writing through Grief

In this writing-intensive class, you'll learn how to write the story of your loss and discover its meaning. You'll create a record of your cherished memories and discover how your loved one is still in your life today. When you complete this class you will have a very special chronicle of your relationship with your loved one.

Class length – 12 weeks   Cost $129

How to Create Your Own Support Group

In this class you will be given assignments that will lead to the creation of your own support group by the completion of the course. You'll decide what type of support group you want to start (online or in-person), create materials to help spread the word and learn how to successfully guide your support group meetings.

Class length – 8 weeks   Cost $79

Basic Strategies and Exercises for Healing

In this interactive, online course, you'll complete 4 different exercises that can help you on your grief journey. You will also learn what to expect on your journey and strategies for coping.

Class length – 3 weeks   Cost $19

**Take a step toward healing.
Enroll today at <u>www.griefsteps.com</u>**

OTHER BOOKS TO HELP YOU ON YOUR JOURNEY...

Grief Steps:
10 Steps to Regroup, Rebuild and Renew After Any Life Loss

by Brook Noel

ISBN 1-891400-35-5
224 pages $14.95

Facing the Ultimate Loss:
Coping with the death of a child

By Robert J. Marx & Susan Davidson

Hardcover 1-891400- 93-2
$23.95
Softcover 1-891400-99-1
$14.95

I Wasn't Ready to Say Goodbye:

Surviving, coping and healing after the sudden death of a loved one

by Brook Noel and Pamela D. Blair, Ph.D.

ISBN 1-891400-27-4
$14.95

also available ...
I Wasn't Ready to Say Goodbye...a companion workbook

ISBN 1-891400-50-9
$18.95

To learn more visit

www.griefsteps.com

Additional books in the GriefGuides Series

Watch for these additional titles being released in 2004. Visit www.griefsteps.com for more information or to place your order

Grief Guides are short, concise guides to assist those who are grieving specific areas in their grief journey. Each GriefGuide is $8.95 US

Surviving Grief: A Compassionate Guide for Your First Year of Grieving

Coping With the Loss of a Partner

Coping With the Loss of a Child

How to Help Someone Who Is Grieving

Surviving Holidays, Birthdays and Anniversaries: Strategies for Coping During Difficult Days

Coping with the Loss of a Sibling

Coping with the Loss of a Parent

Resource and Support for Those Who Are Grieving

Grief Exercises that Help Ease the Pain

Helping Children Cope with Grief

To order any of the products on pages 57-61 by mail, send a check or money order to Champion Press, 4308 Blueberry Road, Fredonia WI 53021. Please include $3.95 shipping and handling for any books ordered and $1 for each additional book. No shipping or handling is necessary for the online classes. Use your visa or mastercard to order online at www.griefsteps.com